The Cus D'Ama__

The simple secrets that took boxers

like Mike Tyson to greatness

From Reemus Boxing

Copyright © 2017 by Rahiem Bailey; Reemus Boxing
All rights reserved.

Independently Published

This book or any portion thereof
may not be reproduced or used in any manner whatsoever
without the express written permission of the publisher
except for the use of brief quotations in a book review.

ISBN 9781549840371

London, United Kingdom

www.ReemusBoxing.com

Introduction

Cus D'Amato was one of a kind. He was a man with revolutionary thoughts regarding the mental aspects of sports. It would be no lie to describe Cus D'Amato as a pioneer in this aspect, teaching the fighters he coached many valuable lessons on life and how to act like a professional.

Cus was known for taking kids right off the street when no one else recognised their inner potential for greatness and success. He took kids from the ghettos and slums of New York, into his home to actually live with him in his 14-room Victorian house in Catskill, New York. This was despite the fact that he didn't even fully know those kids yet.

Cus D'Amato himself understood what it meant to grow up in struggle and pain. His early life experiences definitely solidified the foundation for him to develop the qualities that would later make him famous in the boxing world.

Born on January 17th, 1908, Cus D'Amato grew up in the Bronx, New York City, into an Italian family as the seventh of eight sons.

His father Damiano D'Amato worked as a delivery driver, delivering ice and coal with a horse and cart. Here, Cus D'Amato grew up learning about life on the harsh streets of the Bronx.

As a kid, Cus would see the mobsters trying to force themselves into his father's business. And perhaps this was one of the first lessons Cus learnt that helped to develop him into a leader, as he saw his father stand up to the thugs that tried to intimidate him.

Cus also had the mature consciousness to give himself his best life lessons. At the age of 16, he fasted for four days without food or drink out of choice. He felt that denying himself food and drink would instil in him the ability to cope if mobsters and thugs tried to intimidate him with threats of taking away his livelihood.

This same self-discipline was taken to the Second World War when Cus chose to sleep on the floor, rather than on a bed. He figured that if he could force himself into the harshest and tough environments, he would be confident in any tough situation that would come his way.

At the young age of 25, Cus opened up the Empire Sporting Club with Jack Barrow at The Gramercy Gym, where Cus actually lived for years.

At first, Cus wanted to be 'the next Tony Canzoneri'. But after being left partially blind in one eye from fighting with an older street bully, that was the end of Cus' boxing career. Cus' sole aim became to develop young boxers who would've otherwise been on the streets doing no good. Fate would have it that he would discover and find 3 champions of elite calibre.

What separated, and still does separate, Cus from other fight trainers, is his desire to believe in his fighters. He had an ability to show his fighters why they themselves should believe in their ability. Throughout the years, as his experience and knowledge would grow, so too would his ability to transmit this belief to his boxers.

Cus was a big fan of historical figures and greats, such as Napoleon Bonaparte and Alexander the Great, and he took principles demonstrated from the campaigns of these men as life lessons. He also loved great writers such as Mark Twain, as Twain 'was full of good sense, the sort of good sense that I hope I've been able to transmit to my fighters'.

Cus D'Amato had his first major opportunity to demonstrate his resilience, belief and morality when the notorious IBC mob that controlled the boxing world in the 1950's tried to cut themselves into the contracts of his fighters.

The IBC controlled all of boxing in America, taking charge of the matchmaking, fixing fights and taking large portions of the purses. In a time where no one else had the confidence to stand against them, Cus did.

He refused to allow any promoter that had connections with the IBC to work with his fighters. Eventually, the IBC was shut down after being found to be in violation of the laws, partially because of Cus D'Amato's efforts.

Cus' first famous champion was Floyd Patterson, who broke the record to become the youngest heavyweight champion at the age of just 21. Cus D'Amato took the young boy in at the age of 14, and after years of tutoring Floyd in the art of acting like a champion, as well as fighting with the famous peek-a-boo style, Floyd became a champion.

At the time, Cus showed the inner leader, as he pushed his fighters to fight with a much different style than what was normal. And since Cus' fighters, no boxer has ever fought in the same way with much success.

The revolutionary peek-a-boo style saw fighters hold their hands up high, to their cheeks, while using head movement such as slips and ducks as the primary method of defence.

The head movement would also be used as the foundation for quick counterpunching. Despite this, Cus received much criticism for this, for the simple fact that it was so different. However, the success of the style was solidified by his most famous apprentice, Mike Tyson.

Tyson was brought up with the philosophies of Cus D'Amato in its latest stages, being with the great philosopher in his last few years of life. Cus took Mike from the Tryon detention school for juvenile delinquents to championship glory.

In 1985, Cus died 5 years after he took Mike in, a year before Mike actually became the youngest heavyweight champion at age 20, beating Floyd's record. Despite Tyson's later struggles in life, Cus' mental tips and advice on how to live life and how to be a leader in the boxing world helped to raise Tyson to heights that had not been seen before.

To this day, Cus' philosophies are inspirational to many boxers worldwide. And the argument could easily be made that Cus' approach to life and his focus on character stands alone. Nowhere else, in any sport, does a coach or organisation teach and emphasise the importance of growing and developing your mindset, rather than just your physical skill set.

In this book, we will be covering five concepts of the mental aspect of ring success; character, fear, anxiety, resistance, and leadership. These are areas that a champion-in-training needs to develop if he wishes to realise all of his potential to become truly great.

Solely growing your physical skills are not enough to become a champion. You need to improve your mentality too. We will first present Cus D'Amato's quotes and thoughts regarding each concept. And after that, we will discuss in detail the deeper meanings of what it means to excel mentally in each area.

This book is different to any other boxing book because although it is based on Cus D'Amato, it is written specifically for you. After reading his quotes, we will then discuss the philosophy of his thoughts. We will outline mental instructions and concepts so that you can develop the traits that Cus D'Amato stressed.

Once you have internalised these traits, you will automatically and naturally behave like a champion intuitively with a greater control of your mind and its negative tendencies. Your confidence in your ability, as well as your potential, will grow like never before. We don't all have a great teacher like Cus in life, but we can still profit from his legendary teachings.

Long live Cus D'Amato.

Table of Contents

Table of Contents

- **INTRODUCTION** 3
- **THE CHARACTER OF CHAMPIONS** 10
  - The Philosophy 12
  - The Qualities of a Champion 15
- **FEAR: YOUR FIRE & FRIEND** 36
  - The Philosophy 40
- **ANXIOUS ANTICIPATIONS OF THE ATHLETE** 61
  - Philosophy 64
- **REMARKABLES RISE TO RESISTANCE** 73
  - Philosophy 76
- **LEADERSHIP** 85
  - Philosophy 86
- **CONCLUSION – FINAL NOTES** 96

The Character of Champions

On the importance of having good character traits:

"I'm not a creator. What I do is **discover and uncover**."

"A boy comes to me with a spark of **interest**, I feed the spark and it becomes a flame. I feed the flame and it becomes a fire. **I feed the fire** and it becomes a roaring blaze."

"Boxing is a **contest of character** and ingenuity. The boxer with more **will, determination, desire, and intelligence** is always the one who comes out the victor."

Cus D'Amato believed that the best lessons for life were not simply learnt in the gym. Rather the character defining lessons were developed in everyday life situations:

"I never **teach until I've spoken** to the fighter. I have to first determine his **emotional state**, get his background, to find out what I have to do, how many layers I have to keep peeling off so that I get to the **core of the person** so that he can recognize, as well as I, what is there."

"There is no such thing as a natural puncher. There is a natural aptitude for punching and that is different. **Nobody is born the best. You have to practice and train to become the best.**"

"There are very few new things in this world, very few. That's why people that are young, if they're smart, try to **profit from the experience of an older guy** so they won't have to go through all the pain and suffering. But a certain amount **of pain and suffer is good**, because it makes a person think they've learned"

The Philosophy

Character Is What Makes a Champion

Cus D'Amato was the first, if not one of the first, fight coach to promote the importance of how the mind affects the fighter's performance and the extent of his success within the sport. D'Amato knew that no matter how technically good a fighter is, the primary factor that will determine his ring success is the makeup of his mentality. There are several contributing mental factors that will affect your ability to execute the technical abilities that you learn.

On the other hand, those same mental factors will also affect the fighter's *lack* of ability to implement his physical qualities. Typically, the style, or the ability to punch (and defend) effectively, is only a by-product of a healthy and effective mindset, rather than it being the other way around.

As Cus said 'the physical part of boxing is so minor, that most people would never believe it or accept it. Because, in my opinion, the mind and emotion is about 75% of boxing'. From this perspective, it makes greater sense to focus on the mental aspect, as opposed to the physical aspect. If boxing is 75% mental, is 75% of your energy proportionately dedicated to building great character? If not, you may be harming your potential for success.

The Physical Can Influence the Mental

It is also possible to build championship traits such as confidence *after* operating effectively in the ring, as we have just discussed, rather than the mind initially affecting the physical. On entering the boxing gym, with no confidence, at times, you may see yourself implement a move well and this, in turn, triggers the growth of confidence. However, this actually is still a result of your mind, because as the mind starts to see you executing techniques successfully, it triggers a new realisation for you.

This realisation indicates that it is possible for you to perform these actions with success, which then leads to the championship trait of **belief.** As your belief grows, so does your perception of yourself as a fighter who is able to do more things.

Throughout your attempt for ring success, you will inevitably achieve this realisation not only hundreds but hopefully thousands of times. And each time this happens, as you gain more positive experiences of proof, you build up more mental qualities that spark off a positive cycle of confidence in your ability to win fights.

This confidence will subsequently, of course, lead to you executing more effective actions (such as mastering new techniques and pushing yourself in training), which is imperative for any fighter wishing to gradually transform into a champion.

However, it all starts with your mind. The mind is like a limiting cap that will determine what you are able to execute physically. For this reason, it makes much more sense to dedicate significant amounts of time and efforts towards developing an extremely remarkable mental source of energy.

This is what Cus D'Amato constantly tried to focus on with his fighters and undoubtedly with great results. He created numerous champions; with his most famous students being world champions Mike Tyson, Floyd Patterson, and Jose Torres.

Cus literally took boys from having zero experience and never having fought before, to being Hall of Famers. Other great trainers boast a great list of world champions they worked with, but few of them took their boxers to the zenith of success from when they had no experience at all.

By consistently taking young boys off the street with practically no experience and building them into great fighters, this proves that his results were no fluke. His approach of extreme focus on the mental side of fighting is guaranteed to end in successful results if you do the same.

If you are able to repeat the same process, at least on some level, then you too are giving yourself a better chance of getting the same result. We've said that mental qualities will have a heavy influence on your later success. So what are the specific traits that a fighter should consciously work on?

The Qualities of a Champion

Discipline

As Cus would often say, discipline is the ability to 'do what needs to be done, even when you do not feel like doing it'. We usually expect that our emotional state in the future will always be that of a positive mood. When we first realise that we want to be a fighter, we expect that we will train every day, day in and day out with the same passion we felt when we were motivated. However, this is certainly not the case.

A fighter certainly needs to understand that after the initial period of starting to box, or getting back into training after long periods out, the motivation may not be as intense as it was before. This could be for a number of reasons.

For example, it could be due to the extreme monotony and repetitive nature of working out and practising certain techniques. A fighter masters a technique by doing the exact same thing over and over again. This is guaranteed to get boring.

Or it could be that on certain days, you simply do not feel in the mood, with the draining nature of everyday activities bringing your mood down. Whatever the reason is, a fighter who wishes to be champion of the world must find the discipline to continue to train every day.

A significant reason why discipline is important is due to the fact that mastery of a skill takes time and committed effort to internalise that skill, so that it becomes intuitive. Since boxing requires mastery of many skills, it is as if all fighters are in a race to internalise these skills before the rest. And those who take days off, allow their competitors to get ahead in the race to mastery.

The practical approach to developing discipline is simple. A fighter must make a shift in his thinking. You must understand that a big role which determines how a fighter will perform, is your emotional state at the time. This is why Cus advocated being somewhat emotionless when fighting.

Determining *why* you should perform a certain act (i.e. going for runs early in the morning, going to the gym when you feel tired or frustrated etc.) will allow you to separate emotions from logic. It is easier to get up early in the morning for a run when you shift your focus from how you feel about doing it, to understand that it needs to be done regardless of how you feel. Live by the 'why' of what you're doing, as opposed to whether you feel like doing it.

Tunnel Vision & Focus

A fighter wishing to be a champion needs to prevent himself from wasting away energy to the activities which do not benefit his boxing craft. Only the task of boxing is important. There are many things in this world which can push you off of balance and out of focus. This is particularly the case in this era, with the average person being bombarded with consistent sources of distractions.

If those same sources are helpful to you (including papers, programmes etc.), and help you to progress in boxing, or at least in life, then it can be given the green light. But on the other hand, if those same occupations do not help you, there is little need for it in your life.

Tunnel vision is the fighter's willingness to narrow how his energy is used, putting it into one specific goal. And the more specific the goal is, the better because more energy can be dedicated to the specific task.

A fighter has to become aware of what his desires, expectations and demands are for his future in boxing. What do you wish to get out of boxing? What achievements do you want to earn? Do you want to become world champion? How much money do you want to make? Do you want to become a worldwide superstar, or would you rather be low key? What age seems fit to retire?

You must decisively believe in your answers to any questions you ask yourself. This will allow you to commit to them. Of course, as time goes on, and you progress while becoming aware of your different qualities and preferences, the questions will change and so too will the answers. But it is important that you are always moving towards the established goal.

The next step is establishing how the goal will be achieved. The steps that help you towards this goal should, of course, be done, and any actions that don't help you achieve the desired goal should be considered as a distraction. The distractions for a fighter can come in the form of many things, including friends or people with different agendas, parties and events which take away from time training, girls 'who take so much from you, more than what they give'.

Or it can come from the digital media which distracts you with meaningless visuals for long periods of time. You must limit the time you give towards unproductive activities, and consider it as wasted energy when these activities are done in excess.

The same approach goes for inside of the ring when you are actually fighting in a match. What is the goal? The short term goal may be to throw a specific punch, defend in a certain way, or set up an action like a counter punch.

This is to achieve the obvious long term goal of winning the contest. Any actions which do not serve this objective do not need to take your energy. In the start of a fighter's career, before you know what works and what doesn't, you naturally do many things, some of which helps and some of which doesn't.

As you grow and mature with experience, you start to become aware of what doesn't work, and you discard it accordingly. One such action which is commonly discarded as a fighter gains experience is excessive movement. This may be in the footwork, or in the punches.

For example, as a fighter gets more experienced, his punches become shorter while actually getting more effective and accurate. You start to learn that starting punches from wide angles wastes energy and time. And it is possible to get the same result with even less physical work.

The same goes for foot movement. It is common for fighters to jump around excessively, or move around by taking large steps early on in their careers. Eventually, you learn that you can do much less, to receive the same result of getting into the positions that you want. So the experienced fighter will start to stop himself from bouncing around the ring all of the time, choosing to plant his feet more and save energy.

From this perspective, you can see that tunnel vision can be done both inside the ring and out of it. But it is all for the one purpose of getting closer to boxing mastery. Focus on the objective, constructing the best way possible to achieve it as quickly as possible. Do it without wasting any energy on other unwanted results. This is the aim of tunnel vision and focus.

Adapting & Heart

Being able to adapt to the many different situations that will inevitably challenge you is a trait that is totally necessary if you wish to be a great fighter. When you look at the careers of great fighters, what you will find is that the moments that define them are the toughest scenarios that they either totally overcame, or at least showed strong resistance to before succumbing to the great pressure.

Cus D'Amato strongly believed that the ability to 'rise to the occasion' and become better than the challenge that is presented to you is one of the strongest predictors of a fighter that is destined for success. Confidence in your ability to adapt to different challenges can be built up through consistently putting yourself in challenging situations.

Adapting is directly linked to whether or not you can solve new problems as they arise, finding new solutions. Further difficulty comes in not just trying to decipher the challenge, but to do so while also being under intense amounts of pressure. As you train every day, pushing yourself into new situations despite your fears, you will start to train the muscle in your brain, which is able to think of answers to the new questions you come across.

Cus D'Amato believed that in the scenario that your opponent was technically better than you, the trait of 'heart' could push you to overcome him. This is because the man with more heart will be willing to endure a greater amount of pain and frustration before he decides that he has had enough. This allows him to stay inside that situation long enough to even be in the position to make some sort of comeback. Many times in boxing history, fighters were faced against opponents who had a style that proved to be extremely difficult.

This will continue to happen in the sport's future, and the scenario is inescapable if you are in the sport for a long period of time, pushing yourself to the limit each time. However, having the character trait of heart and the ability to adapt will allow you to defy the odds, as you apply mental pressure to your opponent and force a different result.

To develop this trait, you must keep pushing yourself past your previous limits, in situations which not only require you to work harder, but also to do it with intelligence. This means that the challenging situations must require you to think more logically about how you can overcome the problem. How can you do this?

The most relevant activity for this is sparring. Sparring must be done with a variety of different opponents, with contrasting styles. Fighters often fall in the habit of sparring consistently with the same partner over and over again. But doing this doesn't allow you to run into new problems that you haven't faced before. There is only so much that a specific fighter can come up with. Therefore, you should look to mix up the pack every few weeks, visiting or inviting different types of opponents to your boxing gym to get a better experience at adapting to new scenarios.

Belief & Entitlement

An important aspect of what Cus D'Amato taught his pupils was that it is impossible to become effective in any craft if you do not believe in yourself. Cus believed that this philosophy applied to every single field and industry in the world. This is especially the case in the brutal sport of boxing, where the competition is fierce and the demands on both your mind and body are just as fierce.

The fighter with more belief in his talents and abilities will usually be the one that trains better, performs better and even thinks better. Belief in yourself is about having a high sense of self-worth, believing that you are of enough quality to attract positive results. You must know that there is no reason why you shouldn't be able to get the things that you want out of life, and in the ring.

When you think about it and look back at boxing history, literally hundreds of men have done enough to earn the right to be mentioned in the Hall of Fame. This doesn't mean that the feat is an easy one. But it does put it into perspective. The task is certainly not an impossible one. This means that it isn't illogical at all to make the statement that you will achieve this too. In fact, it makes total sense that if you follow the same process of hard and smart work that the past and current greats underwent, then you too will get the same results.

Belief starts from the desire to be a champion. As you start to put in more action and get more experience, the desire starts to become backed by belief. This means that in the earliest stages of your career before you have the positive experiences to logically justify having a belief in your ability to perform as a great boxer, you will need to couple your desire with (somewhat irrational) affirmations.

This simply means you will need to tell yourself that you are a champion, even before it happens. And it is only considered irrational from the perspective that it isn't reflected in the outer world yet. Only you can see it at this point.

However, deep within your mind, this belief that you will be champion is true. As you start to gain the successes and experiences that reflect this, the belief will become more tangible. And when you get to the point where you have the experiences to match the positive affirmations you tell yourself, the belief becomes even more stable.

These beliefs can become concrete to the point that even if you wanted to talk your ability down, it would be extremely difficult for you to even believe it. This means that it becomes difficult for any challenge or critic to knock your belief down too.

Without belief, it is not possible to imagine yourself being able to perform effectively as a fighter. And if your mind cannot harbour positive expectations about what type of results you can get on a consistent basis, then it would make no sense for you to be motivated to get those results.

As previously noted, building up a mental catalogue of positive experiences in the ring will make your belief more concrete. However, by also being aware of the positive qualities that you have, it becomes easier for you to believe in your abilities.

For example, ask yourself what are the physical advantages that you have compared to other boxers? This will increase your sense of belief in influencing a certain outcome. Are you strong? Are you quick? Are you able to remain cool under pressure? Do you have good stamina?

Everyone has different advantages. Acknowledging and embracing these qualities, you will help strengthen your self-belief, as you gather more evidence to support this belief. With belief, a fighter will remain resilient in the face of threats. This is due to a sense of entitlement that you are the type of fighter who deserves the positive outcome.

It will become more natural to you to expect that you are the type of person who deserves a winning result. So when you need to adapt, then you can do so for a longer period of time, with a greater amount of expectation as you search for various ways to win. Belief will prevent you from giving up, as it will seem illogical to you that there isn't a way that you can find a way to win the fight. Entitlement assumes that you are going to find a way to win, no matter the circumstances.

Openness & Receptiveness

Essential to Cus' approach to tutoring fighters, was his 'teachings' about life, character, and the inner game of being an athlete. For you to even benefit from this, a fighter has to be open to the idea of even developing his mind, just as much as he develops his body.

For most of the boxing world, the inner game of fighting is overlooked and placed as the secondary factor in fighting, as opposed to the other way around. For the fighters that were able to buy into his ideas, believing that what he had to say was of benefit rather than harm, they were able to progress significantly.

On the other hand, a fighter who cannot believe in the knowledge that is being laid right before his very eyes and ears will fail to progress as quickly as the former. This approach to being open applies to every area of training and progress. You must seek out new information from a variety of sources.

Never discard a source as one which you cannot learn from. By being receptive to more sources for information, you will allow yourself to be in a constant state of progress. This will move you closer to your goal every single day without fail. You must find a way to make the environment give you more quality and feedback than it does to your competitors.

How can you extract more quality out of a situation, than it gives to your rivals, despite it being the exact same situation?

One method is by simply listening more. Cus strongly believed that valuable time and pain (of effort and failure) could be saved by simply allowing yourself to be mentored by those with more experience than you. When you are in the gym, and you are receiving feedback from your trainer, you have to concentrate on what it is that he is saying fully. And if there is something you do not understand fully, ask for clarification or an alternative explanation. However, listening doesn't extend to just your trainer. It extends to *everyone*. And by everyone, that includes people who may seem less able than you in the ring.

For example, casual spectators and those boxing advisors in your gym who are not your trainers. By taking in information from more sources than your opponent, you are able to progress more quickly. A fighter should also ask many, many questions. And he should be very open to the possibility that all answers could be correct, even if he doesn't initially think so.

Many fighters are in gyms where there are older people who have a wealth of experience in the fight game, but they never ask questions that could help them improve. This is a great loss for those fighters when you consider that most people are ready and willing to give away the information that they have. Make a rule that every day you are in the gym, you will come up with a new question to ask each time.

Questions may be based on different methods of training, or eating habits, or perhaps the technical intricacies of how a punch should be thrown. It doesn't necessarily matter if not every question is the perfect one. What matters more is that you just ask any question, and progress a little bit, as opposed to not at all.

Another major problem for fighters is observation. A lot can be learnt from simply observing other fighters, and how the other fighter's trainers teach. The reason this is a problem for fighters is because it is difficult to spend long periods of time watching others in the gym when you yourself are working out.

But if you are able to open your mind to the capabilities of other fighters, then you can make links between the results that they have and what they mechanically do to get those results. If you have been training for long periods and can feel your energy (or focus) levels dropping, then it may make better sense to take a short break and observe instead.

However, to make it productive, you should immediately mimic the actions that you are watching, so that you start to know how you can do it, as opposed to simply how it looks. By always listening, asking, and observing, you can be in a state of permanent progress, always getting better much more quickly than other fighters.

Goal Orientated & Winning Drive

One of the biggest things that separate the champions who consistently win and the challengers who consistently accept the possibility of loss is the amount to which the fighter fixates on the outcome. The entire set up of Cus D'Amato's approach was so that the fighter could rationally have reason to place victory in his head as not just a priority, but also an expectation. Many fighters are much too open and okay with the possibility of defeat. Hence, they are much more likely to lose because it is an acceptable outcome for them in their reality.

For ambitious champions, losing is an outcome which must be harshly rejected. Cus D'Amato would instil in his fighters the mantra 'refuse to lose'. When training and leading up to the fight, it is important that you imagine clearly yourself being victorious. This is especially the case when you put many hours in because you've given yourself a reason to justify that you have earned the right to win logically.

It could be argued that Cus D'Amato stressed being victorious to the point that he was trying to create a megalomaniac. He attempted to create the 'perfect' fighter. With Mike Tyson, Cus instilled in him the necessity of winning.

And the winning wasn't to be done in an okay fashion. Rather, he believed that his fighters should win magnificently, dramatically knocking out their opponents and entertaining the crowd while doing so. This is reflected in the 'peek-a-boo' style that he taught to his fighters, which was developed to enhance a fighter's ability to instantly counterpunch his opponents and score with flash punches from awkward positions.

To enhance the extent to which his fighters set their eyes on victory, Cus would set up the importance of victory in an irrational way. Victory wasn't just about winning the boxing match, but it was for an even higher purpose. For example, winning the championship title was an important 'mission', which the world needed to see. If the world couldn't see it then, as Mike Tyson later described 'civilisation would end as we know it'.

Cus also repeated over and over again to Tyson that he wasn't just an average boxer, but a descendant of the sport's greatest champions, like Jack Dempsey or Joe Louis. He even preached to him that he was of the same blood of history's greatest conquerors such as Alexander the Great and Napoleon Bonaparte. From this perspective, winning is more than just how the average person perceives winning. Winning is a mission that has to be achieved by any means necessary. Nothing must be allowed to prevent the outcome from coming to fruition.

For many fighters, it may be difficult to place these types of beliefs in your head, especially if you are not surrounded by an environment where these types of statements would be considered as even remotely sane. However, it is still possible to develop a fixation on winning to at least almost the same degree. You must also set the task of attaining victory to a higher purpose. The purpose should be one that makes more sense to you.

So for example, instead of perceiving the win as a task from the heavens, you can perceive the necessity of winning as one which will eventually inspire. The people who you could inspire might be hundreds, if not thousands, of young kids who may look up to you.

Instead of perceiving yourself as a descendant of Alexander the Great, you can still choose to repetitively affirm to yourself that you are the chosen one in your neighbourhood or country. For someone chosen, winning is a necessity. This means it must be a necessity for you if you wish to fill that role. If you do not feel as though you are worth the consistent wins, then you are unlikely to win as consistently as you could.

Despite the fact that Cus D'Amato put a great emphasis on winning, he also believed that losing shouldn't have a massive effect on your mind. This means that you shouldn't put too much importance on losing if it does happen. Generally, fighters and athletes often make the mistake of attaching their identity to a loss that they've endured. Cus told his fighters that they should 'never take it personal', if they took a loss.

Ultimately, it is possible for a winner to endure a loss and still be considered as acting like a winner. A loss (or even a win) doesn't define who you are as a man outside of the ring. And a loss is only a loss 'if nothing is learnt from it'.

If you happen to lose a match, you must act as the winner would in that situation. Someone who is a winner in all situations would take as much value from the 'losing' situation as possible. This is so that you can come back from the event stronger than when you went in. This is how you can transform situations into win-win. Regardless of what the outcome is, you've turned the ultimate ending into the most positive one that you could have.

Process Orientated & Passion

Being process orientated is in contrast to being result oriented. But it is important that you find the balance between the two. The path to the championship is a task that cannot be completed quickly. It takes many, many years to achieve the ultimate objective of winning a championship title. This is where the importance of patient passion comes in, as it will be the fuel that allows you to remain motivated for years and years.

Being passionate about boxing is about loving the actual process itself. And while being results orientated is important as we've already discussed, only focusing on the end goal will always make it seem too far in the future. It will be hard to remain motivated if you only look at the long term result. There needs to be a balance between process orientation and results orientation. Focusing on the win influences the direction and intention of what you do. However, focusing on the process influences the energy which you need to even move in that direction.

Cus D'Amato highly rated young fighters who demonstrated intense levels of interest in the sport. He believed that the amount of interest a fighter had could be considered as the initial measure of how far a fighter would be willing to buy into the reality of giving boxing all of their efforts. Drawing on your passion for the sport will allow you to take your role as a learner to extreme heights.

Again, using Mike Tyson as an example, Cus D'Amato raved about Mike's enthusiasm for boxing, noting that the young Tyson was hugely excited about the prospect of fighting at all times of the day. This meant the potential costs of training, such as time used, sacrifices suffered, negative emotions experienced and the physical pains were viewed as minor expenses.

The end result of winning and acquiring championship belts are not the only things that can be seen as benefits. When you enjoy the actual process of going to training, punching the bag, running the miles and sparring, the entire experience before the end is enjoyable too. This is also important because even when you win a contest or win a certain championship, if you are strictly results orientated, you risk potentially becoming demotivated after you reach that goal.

For example, if you fixate on become world champion, using this as your sole primary motivator for years, what will motivate you once you have won the championship? Rather, if you also put emphasis on the process, theoretically you can be permanently motivated.

Confidence

A consistent core trait of all highly skilled fighters who are great is confidence. Confidence allows a fighter to keep himself from making the event bigger than his capabilities. Champions recognise their value to the world, and specifically their own ability to perform.

Without confidence, it is impossible for you to have clarity of intent and conviction in your actions, inside the ring and in life. Cus D'Amato believed that if a fighter did not have confidence in his abilities and his own sense of self-worth, then there was no way that he could execute the strategies and tactics that he had learnt in the gym.

It is inevitable that when you are faced with difficult periods in your life, you will be prone to doubts and worries. You will wonder whether you are fooling yourself into trying to convince yourself that you are able to become a champion, or even win against a certain opponent. This is somewhat normal. And as long as you are confident in yourself and in your skills, those negative thoughts will always be momentary, rather than being permanent.

Confidence in your skills can be grown by building up enough positive experiences in a certain activity. This encourages you into thinking that you are a master at a particular set of techniques. By practising a certain move repeatedly, you start to get better at it and believe more that the desired outcome will come to fruition. And repeating it in a number of different situations will only serve to increase your confidence in the technique as you see how it brings you favourable results.

If you work for hours and hours on your footwork, mastering the art of escaping onslaughts from your opponent or stepping out of range, it will be easy for you to be put into a situation which requires this defensive footwork. You will execute it quickly and effectively. If not, you will question whether you can do it effectively. The mental effort and time it takes to question yourself will give your opponent the split second that he needs to possibly land a punch and make a difference in the fight.

General confidence in your own character is also essential. Without it, it will be impossible to commit to any physical action enough for it to make a difference to the match. For example, a fighter who isn't self-confident could easily be forced into a deeper state of anxiety and hesitation by simply taking the walk to the ring with hundreds of eyes watching. Inevitably, this would harm the fighter's performance.

However, a confident fighter doesn't let those same outside external factors influence what his own emotional state is inside. This grants him the special prerogative to act logically when he starts fighting. His performance will remain in alignment with what he believes he can do, and what he is actually capable of doing.

Learn & Develop

It is important that all of these traits are consistently and permanently developed upon. There are no championship traits that cannot be developed to improve your inner game. Failure to develop them for long periods of time will diminish your ability to train and perform as effectively as you can. The actions of a champion have to be sustained over a long period of time, over the course of years. This means that you have to become a champion at the deepest parts of your core, performing as an ambitious elite fighter intuitively and automatically, rather than temporarily acting like one.

Traits such as focus and openness are easily sustained when a fighter is driven by his 'spark of interest'. Extreme enthusiasm isn't simply about loving to train and fight in the sport of boxing. But it also means a fighter loathes the time that he does not spend in the sport of boxing, finding it difficult to stay away.

With high levels of enthusiasm, it should be painful and frustrating for a fighter to not be progressing, or learning. Passion for the sport will allow you to sustain your motivation when times are difficult and challenging.

After overcoming the obstacles that life deals you, your resilience grows. Consequently, you place yourself in an upwards spiral of confidence and positivity. A great champion needs to learn how to control, dictate and assess his own emotions. As you grow and develop the traits of a quality champion, you will inevitably become better at managing your own mind and emotions.

A fighter with his emotions out of his control will fail to perform to his full potential. There are many outside factors that will threaten to impact your abilities and emotions. The situations you experience will differ. This could refer to the different opponents you will face, the judges you will fight in front of, the referees that do your bout and the crowds that watch you. However, the factor which doesn't have to change is you and your attitude to these different scenarios.

Wider society and even the general boxing world gives the impression that success and championship status is given to you when you are born into the world. The world would have you believe that you are either born with greatness, or you are not. The media portrays the idea that you are either talented or doomed. And by these accounts, if you are not born confident and strong-willed, you need to simply to accept your fate of mediocrity and live an average life.

However, this is not the case, and Cus D'Amato understood that we are all born on a generally level playing field. He 'didn't believe in talent'. And even when some fighters are naturally talented, or show that certain techniques come easier to them, the talent differences can be outweighed by demonstrating the qualities of a champion. Success is a marathon, not a sprint.

Cus D'Amato believed that we all have greatness within us, and we all certainly have the potential to grow as you gain experience. The sole issue is only 'uncovering' and 'peeling away the layers' which prevents you from being in touch with that greatness. What you believe you are not, holds you back more so than what you believe you are.

The many different people and groups that we encounter from a young age tend to encourage us to believe that there is more reason to not think of yourself as a champion, rather than one. And for this reason, we must work on stripping away these false and untrue influences, so that we start to see the naked and true quality that has always been there.

Fear: Your Fire & Friend

Cus on the lack of focus on the importance of fear in the boxing world:

"A fighter has to **know fear**."

"Fear is the greatest obstacle to learning in any area, but particularly in boxing.

For example, boxing is something you learn through repetition. You do it over and over and suddenly you've got it."

"However, in the course of trying to learn, if you get hit and get hurt, this makes you cautious, and **when you're cautious you can't repeat it** [the action]

And when you can't repeat it, it's going to **delay the learning process**."

"When they come up to the gym and say I want to be a fighter, the first thing I'd do was talk to them about fear."

"**Fear is a protective mechanism**. By talking to the fighters about **fear I cut the learning time maybe by as much as half**, sometimes more, depending on the individual."

"I would always use the same example of the deer crossing an open field and upon approaching the clearing suddenly instinct tells him danger is there, and nature begins the survival process, which involves the body releasing adrenalin into the bloodstream, causing the heart to beat faster and enabling the deer to perform extraordinarily feats of agility and strength.

It enables the deer to get out of range of the danger, helps him escape to the safety of the forest across the clearing. An example in which fear is your friend."

"The thing a kid in the street fears the most is to be called yellow or chicken, and sometimes a kid will do the most stupid, wild, crazy things just to hide how scared he is.

I often tell them that while fear is such an obnoxious thing, an embarrassing thing, nevertheless **it is your friend**.

Because anytime anyone saves your life perhaps a dozen times a day, no matter what how obnoxious he is, you've got to look upon him as a friend, and this is what fear is."

"Since **nature gave us fear in order to help** us survive, we **cannot look upon it as an enemy**.

Just think how many times a day a person would die if he had no fear. He'd walk in front of cars, he'd die a dozen times a day."

"A boy comes to me and tells me that he's not afraid, if I believed him I'd say he's a liar or there's something wrong with him.

I'd send him to a doctor to find out what the hell's the matter with him, because this is not a normal reaction."

"The fighter that's gone into the ring and hasn't experienced fear is either a liar or a psychopath."

"**Every fighter that ever lived had fear.**"

"**Boxing is a sport of self-control**. You must understand fear so you can **manipulate it**. "

"Fear is like fire. You can **make it work for you**: it can warm you in the winter, cook your food when you're hungry, give you light when you are in the dark, and produce energy.

Let it go out of control and it can hurt you, even kill you."

On the importance of managing your psychology as you get in the ring:

"When two men step into the ring, one and **only one deserves to win**. When you step into the ring, **you gotta know you deserve** to win.

You gotta know destiny owes you victory, **because you trained harder** than your opponent. You sparred harder. You ran farther."

"The next thing I do, I **get them in excellent condition**. Knowing how the **mind is and the tricks it plays** on a person and how an individual will always look to avoid a confrontation with something that is intimidating, I remove all possible excuses they're going to have before they get in there."

"The man who has the **confidence that his ability will not be denied**, especially when you **know what your ability is**, nobody can con you"

"By getting them in **excellent condition, they can't say when they get tired** that they're not in shape.

When they're in excellent shape I put them into the ring to box for the first time, usually with an experienced fighter who won't take advantage of them.

When the novice throws punches and nothing happens, and his opponent keeps coming at him, the **new fighter becomes panicky**.

When he gets panicky he wants to quit, but he can't quit because his whole psychology from the time he's first been in the streets is to condemn a person who's yellow. So what does he do? **He gets tired**."

"This is what happens to fighters in the ring. They get tired. They get tired, because they're getting afraid.

Now that he gets tired, people can't call him yellow. He's just too "tired" to go on.

But let that same fighter strike back wildly with a visible effect on the opponent and suddenly that tired, exhausted guy becomes a tiger. It's **a psychological fatigue**, that's all it is.

But people in boxing don't understand that."

"Fear is a friend of exceptional people."

The Philosophy

Ground-Breaking Approach to Fear

Cus' famous philosophies and thoughts on fear are revolutionary. Seldom before had boxing coaches ever speak of fear in the same manner as Cus D'Amato did. Even to this day, there are few fight coaches that can relay the message to their fighter that fear can be used to your benefit.

Cus emphasised to his fighters that fear could be limited. It doesn't have to hinder your performance. He believed that a fighter who operates with the fear of being hit actually increases his chances of this reality. This is because he has emitted a thought and vision in his head, in much the same way that a fighter with belief does.

The boxer who allows his fear to rage out of control, allowing it to spark off limiting beliefs in his mind, opens himself up to the possibility of failing. Specifically, the fighter may have a fear of failing to accomplish his desired outcome inside of the ring.

In much the same way that a fighter with belief feels entitled to a winning result, the fearful fighter feels his worth (in that situation at least) is deserved of a scenario which may include him failing to receive the win that he wants.

These are the inner issues which Cus D'Amato felt he needed to address, even before his fighters stepped into the ring. If not, it would have been near impossible for that fighter to take advantage of his potential. As highlighted before, Cus D'Amato didn't teach any technical skills to his fighters before he had the chance to speak to them about the mental issues that they would face.

Dealing with Fear

Failing to speak to the fighters would mean that certain concepts would also fail to resonate with the fighter. This is down to the fact that those certain thoughts or suggestions that Cus would make wouldn't be perceived as being possible for him in his reality. Therefore the fighter would simply discard what he was taught. Or perhaps the fighter wouldn't agree with the logic of what Cus was teaching him to do if they still harboured a *feeling* of fear about what could happen if they did what he was suggesting.

However, by eliminating the major hindrance of (excessive) fear, Cus' fighter could choose to believe in the potential for success of the technical suggestion. Thus it would be possible for them to do it. Illustrating this philosophy was how Cus taught his fighters to fight in the ring. Cus strongly believed in the saying that boxing is about 'hitting, and not getting hit'. He taught his fighters to get into positions, via intelligent footwork and swift head movement, so that the fighter was in the better position to abide by that saying.

If a fighter was able to step over to the blind side of his opponent, it would make much more sense to the fighter that he is safely permitted to throw a punch with 'bad intentions'. This fighter, in a relatively safe position, can now fully commit to the blow with all of his weight and his focus. This is because he knows logically that it is unlikely that he will be hit in return. The fear of being hit, which is naturally one of the biggest fears that a fighter may have, is dramatically lowered in this situation.

Even more than just limiting fear, Cus also uniquely acknowledged that fear can actually be used in your favour. Fear, from a positive perspective, can be seen as a friendly tool that can be used to propel a fighter to greater heights.

This is opposite to the seemingly common perspective that fear should be something to ignore. The truth is that it is highly unlikely that you will ever erase fear totally from your life. Nor will this belief about fear ever be productive for you. The risk will still be there, so it's better to switch your perspective of it to one that is more beneficial.

Absolutely everything that is a part of your life should be made to somehow work in your favour. This is whether you perceive it as an obstacle (such as an uncomfortable emotion etc.) or not. If you allow fear to exist in your life uncontrolled, it will simply be a 'cost' to you. Uncontrolled, it is an emotion that decreases your abilities, rather than adding to it. With this in mind, it is much more logical and productive to make use of it, since it's going to be prevalent in your life anyway.

Cus' approach to fear abides by this principle by making the most out of an emotion that usually would stifle and limit the fighter. Unmanaged fear not only stifles the level of the performance for a fighter, but it also decreases the extent of his progression and learning curve in training when he encounters failures and painful experiences.

D'Amato believed that, depending on the fighter, if you are able to control, manage or at least understand your fears, then you will dramatically quicken the time it takes for you to learn new skills. Fear prevents them from doing, what they know in their head they would like to do, and what they know they actually could do if they put their efforts to it.

A fearful fighter or 'coward' will run when he encounters obstacles. However, a fighter who has managed his fear, or a 'hero', will still persist in spite of fear being there. Cus understood that for the most part, fear could actually be extremely healthy and productive. It keeps us from putting ourselves in serious danger. As he said, without fear 'we'd walk into the road and get hit by cars', and we'd be reckless versions of ourselves. Fear keeps us in check.

However, the problem comes when fear starts to hold us back from what we can actually achieve, even if it meant suffering a little bit of pain. For example, in order to get good at new techniques in the ring, you will have to balance the costs of actually failing and getting countered, with the benefits of eventually learning to do it successfully.

When we try the new technique we want to use in sparring; it is likely that we will fail and suffer some sort of pain (via the counter). But it makes sense that as long as the pain is short term, this is a small price to pay for the benefit. Managing fear can help you separate yourself from your boxing competitors because fear will surely hold back a significant amount of boxers who want to try new things. You can make the difference in progress, by shedding yourself of these fears.

Fear starts to become irrational and uncontrollable after we suffer from real intense pains. These pains relate to traumatic experiences, such as losing a fight we badly wanted to win or humiliation in front of large audiences when attempting certain feats. As a consequence, we are often left with mental scars that cause us pain. This mental pain carries the triggers to feelings of anxiety, as we fear feeling what we previously felt when we went through the uncomfortable experience. And we are afraid to then perform with the same levels of enthusiasm.

However, if we do not perform with that same level of commitment, we slow our rate of progress, because we are less engaged and conscious. To gain new skills in boxing, your mind needs to feel free of anything potentially holding it back. Knowing this, you must learn to exclude excessive levels of fear. As a champion, you must befriend fear, learning how to use it in your favour and to your advantage.

Rationalising Fear

Cus D'Amato perhaps was the best boxing trainer in history, when it came to totally transforming his fighters' perspectives on fear. Luckily, the capability to do so isn't limited to just his fighters of the 20th century. By repeating the process, using the same mental methods, we can repeat the results for ourselves.

Many fighters, who are ambitious and often dream of their future success, still lack actual control of their mind and knowledge of how it works. In much the same way that Cus didn't teach his fighters before speaking to them, you have to assess your own mental state. You need to know specifically what your fears are. If you don't know what your fears are, then it is impossible for you to change them or do anything about it.

Once you are aware, then you can start to establish how all of these fears can be made to work for you. And if they cannot be shifted in your favour, you must do either two things: you must label the fear as unproductive and look to find a way to get rid of it or find a way to work in spite of it.

It becomes easier to accept fear when we acknowledge that every fighter in history had fear inside him too. This includes your greatest fighters, such as Muhammad Ali or Roberto Duran. And these were men that were viewed as fearless. However, acting fearless doesn't necessarily mean that there was a total absence of the emotion. Rather it meant that the fear was able to be controlled by the fighter.

One way of managing how you feel about fear is by starting to change what you think about it. One of the simplest of ways to do this is by rationalising fear. This is so that it becomes a familiar friend in our minds, rather than an intrusive enemy which we seek to eliminate.

The harsh, and near-impossible, task of trying to eliminate fear is unlikely to work. And in the process, you risk inducing yourself with even more negative feelings, such as tension. If you wish to change how fear encourages or discourages, you, you must start to change your perspective.

It is difficult to perceive fear as something negative once you understand that at the root, it isn't meant to harm us. Rather, it is meant to keep us safe and alive. After switching our perspective with logic, we then can consciously decide to perform despite the existence of fear in our mind. And if a fighter can change the way fear exists in his mind, this will change the way the biological chemicals of fear are felt in his body.

By rationalising fear, we learn to relax and avoid excessive tensions in our muscles even if fear is still present. And in this relaxed state, it makes it easier to enter the zone, where the mind is more productive. This will make it less likely for you to get tired in a fight, and the blows that you receive will seem to have less of an impact.

Fear magnifies the shock value of a punch in your own mind because it will cause you to focus more on the prospect of what it is that you fear. And the more you focus on this negative outcome, the more you believe it to be true even before it happens.

More importantly, as you visualise and believe in the negative outcome, you automatically lose focus from the being able to imagine the winning outcome coming true. In other words, the more you fear, the more you actually manifest your own defeat, all because of the fact that fear was allowed to run rampant in your mind.

For example, one of the biggest predictors of when a fighter has given up on getting the win is when he starts to become passive in his punching. More importantly, it is the emotional blockages that prevent him from being able to punch freely and often.

As the fighter starts to punch less and less, it will often be the case that he brings his guard up in a very passive manner (as opposed to trying to actively respond to each punch as it comes). When this happens, the fighter is telling his opponent through his body language, that he is focusing more on the potential scenario of being punched, rather than on doing the punching.

It is highly unlikely for a fighter who believes in his chances of winning the fight for him to demonstrate physically (by being passive in both offence and defence) that he is willing to give up the initiative. So rounds later when the passive fighter is knocked out, or the ref has stopped the fight, spectators get the impression that the fight was decided at that moment. Rather, it is likely that in many situations, the winner of the fight was decided long before that, as they mentally jousted and subconsciously negotiated who it is that will leave the ring as the winner.

So if you have an excessive focus on the fear of losing, then each time you are hit, you are increasing the likelihood that your focus will shift to the negative prospects that you have. Not only will your body language become passive, but as Cus taught, the fighter will start to subtly look for ways out of the fight. This could be by 'allowing' himself to get tired, which could be argued is more a case of him simply focusing on the fatigue. It could also be by resorting to strategies which are more basic and lazy, as he struggles to implement what he has learnt in recent weeks and months.

When the mind isn't being weighed down by fearful inhibitions, you are able to do so much more. This includes the luxury of being able to think more quickly under pressure. And in this way, your thinking isn't biased towards the potential negative outcome. Rather it is realistic about future events and even optimistic.

Taking it further, if we do not resist fear, we can allow fear to propel us to greater strengths, as we use certain rational fears as mental motivation. This means that there are actually a number of fears that are in alignment with our targets. By shifting your focus on fear to these 'positive' rationalisations on fear, you start to turn fear into your 'best friend', as Cus D'Amato described it.

What Are Some Friendly Fears That You Should Have?

As an ambitious fighter, you should have the **fear of performing to less than your potential** and losing as a result of this. The aim of having this fear is so that you have no mental blockages that stop you from fully diving into what it is that you want to accomplish. This is better than having the fear of giving your all but wasting your energy on something that doesn't work out.

It is somewhat natural for us to think of a plan B to boxing, or imagine the reality that we can waste our time and effort by training in this sport, and it doesn't go as we imagine it. It may initially seem counter-intuitive, but this will do more harm then it will do you good.

The problem with this mindset is that it is unlikely that you will do anything with the proper engagement that is required to do it well. With this mentality, it is certainly impossible to do whatever it is you want to do well enough so that you become the best at it. Somewhere else in the sport, there will be another fighter who dives fully into his boxing. And he will be the one who deserves ring success more than you.

In order to conquer this fear, you must accept the reality that it's possible to commit to boxing and come up short. However, by accepting it, you give yourself license to fully engage with, which actually makes it much less likely that you will fail in what is that you want to do. Now you can be focused, rather than diverting your energy in different things.

You could also relate this to the **fear of wasting your youth**. One day when you are old and less able to act on your desires, you will look back and hope that you have no regrets. The best time to act on your youthful energy is now. This is for fear that you will look back on your life, wishing that you made the most of the opportunity you had. This idea of needing to commit fully is also applicable to the actual fighting itself.

When you throw a punch, if you are scared of stepping and committing weight to that punch, for fear that you might miss or get countered, then your punch will be half-hearted. You will not step into the punch properly. This will mean you will fail to hurt your opponent *and* you'll also give him a better chance of countering you.

Even further, you will have wasted valuable energy, going against the fear that you had initially (which was to not waste time or energy).

Another issue that cripples many fighters is the fear of potentially being humiliated when failing to do something in the ring as good as you imagined you would do it. Rather, this **fear of being humiliated should actually push you to invest** more time and effort into trying to master that certain skill. If you don't want an opponent to potentially humiliate you, then build up a skillset that would prevent this from happening.

At first, it is impossible to expect that you will be able to get good at rare techniques without failing. If it were easy to have unique skills, then everyone would. Naturally, the way of a champion is to try and attain the more ambitious goal, which inevitably means greater risk.

If you wish to limit the extent to which the risk becomes a reality, then you must commit to training even harder than you otherwise would have. It has to become the norm for you, to practice your skills repeatedly in a way that most other fighters wouldn't.

You must train harder and longer than your rivals and peers, and this will reduce the risk of being humiliated by failures when it is match time. This shifts this particular fear into your accomplice, helping to push you to greater success.

Another major fear which threatens entire fight careers is the fear of finances, specifically the lack of it if you pursue boxing. As they put all their energy into boxing, many fighters will struggle until they have 'made it' to stardom. Inevitably, the temptation to get a reliable job may be there. However, **the fear of struggling financially is the perfect motivation** to train astronomically hard.

Luckily, the fighters of Cus D'Amato were able to actually live with him, as he lived in a 14 room mansion in the Catskills. Fighters, such as Mike Tyson, who were living in the house, had less pressure to go out and get a normal 9-5 job.

You may be one of the many fighters who does not have the luxury of not having to worry about finances as you progress with your boxing career. Many fighters find themselves having to choose a more stable career, because of the fact that their financial situation is not promising.

However, you can find inspiration from the fact that most of the sport's greatest fighters came from poverty-stricken environments where the next meal would sometimes be a mystery. Yet they managed to use this hunger and fear of poverty, to encourage themselves to be rich and successful.

If you are in a position where you desperately want to be financially safe, then this is all the more reason for you to focus on boxing with no distractions. The risk of failure is too costly. Going to the boxing gym every day, or at least training every day is a requirement if you are in a situation where you need to make money. You need to technically progress even quicker than your rivals so that you can progress in the paid ranks. This allows you to turn the fear of poor finances into your favour.

This is also the case for the **healthy fear of fearing to provide for and inspire your family**. A fighter with relatives who look up to him for financial support or even life guidance should have the fear of not being able to provide this. This should help him to find even greater levels of discipline and motivation.

For fighters who are fans of boxing history or great historical figures in general, the **fear of being forgotten can motivate you** to want to make history and leave a legacy. If you are to create history, then you have to do something that not many people in history have done before.

A task of this great magnitude requires a great deal of training to be done. Even more than that, you must be consistently putting yourself in difficult positions which others would be too afraid to do. These challenging positions will aid your progress, more than any timid attempts at trying new things.

It is very possible that you are one of the many fighters as if the ring is a place of expression, giving you a stage to showcase character and personality to the world. This is especially the case for kids that grow up in environments where they struggle to express themselves socially.

If you're a fighter who can relate to this, then you should have the **fear of not being able to express your truest nature in the ring,** if you do not box. This will motivate you to appreciate the opportunity to fight.

Millions, if not billions, of people around the globe, lack the knowledge of what their passion or talent is. The fact that you are even aware that boxing is your passion, let alone the fact that you have the opportunity to have it as your career should be a reason for great gratitude.

The fear of losing this opportunity (and privilege) to demonstrate your passionate side in such a sport should encourage you to appreciate the chance to train and fight. If you procrastinate and waste time, it may be the case that you get injured one day, or endure another situation that forces you to stop boxing. If this happens, you will wish that you took full advantage of the time you had to make the most of the sport.

These are among some of the legitimate fears that you could have, that if you embrace, can give you reasons to commit more energy, belief and dedication to your craft. And this is what many fighters fail to do, hence why many fighters will fail to realise their full potential or become great professionals inside the ring.

...rs of Losing: Sacrifice

...est characteristics of Cus D'Amato's approach to ...ighters for long term success was sacrifice. Sacrifice is an ...y motivational drive. It can push you to a result in the situations ...ch require you to be more than what you are on the surface. It helps you dig deeper. And you need this capability if you wish to be great.

Sacrifice on a long term basis, over the course of years, is a difficult ask for a fighter. This is the case no matter how ambitious he is. You must 'give up what you feel is important, for a cause that you feel is more important'. This can only be done through discipline, a trait that Cus D'Amato often raved about.

Your emotions may discourage you from what you *know* you must do. But you must 'do what you hate to do, in the same manner as if you loved to do it'. And then every accomplishment and cheque you receive will be greatly deserved.

As previously noted, fears are a normal part of an ambitious fighter's life in the sport. Aside from the fears that prevent you from training and progressing as quickly as you can, the main fear which intrudes a fighter's mind is the fear of losing. Of course, this fear is mostly significant leading up to an actual match, in the weeks before a fight right up until the moments before the bell rings.

The fear of actually losing leads to doubts and worries. And this discourages the fighter from believing in himself and his own prospect of winning. Sacrifice is about making sure that the doubts that you have are unjustified.

Excessive fear of losing prior to a match can be eliminated, or at least limited, by giving your mind evidence. The evidence is the proof your mind needs to truly abandon any excuses which are of no use to you. As the fear of losing is sown weeks before the fight, the remedy is to start preventing this weed from growing.

You do this by simply investing in the prospect of your victory, to the extent that you truly believe the most logical result that could happen is your win. As Cus D'Amato said, you need to go into the ring 'knowing you were destined to win'. The result needs to be a 'foregone conclusion' that fate preordained even before you stepped into the ring.

The fear of losing can be limited by going through many different training experiences that result in a substantial amount of productive 'pain'. The result of this pain is that a fighter will achieve a unique state of confidence, which is detached from overly obsessing about a potential loss.

Through this, you won't feel the need to take winning or losing as what defines who you are. 'Winning, losing, never take it personal', Cus D'Amato would say. At the same time, however, you will still be fully engaged and attached to performing to the best of your abilities. This is because you will be without any limiting doubts. This approach allows a fighter to feel in more control about his own outcome.

But also at the same time, it allows him to feel that whether he wins or not, there wasn't much else he could've done. Then he won't have to experience any guilt in the aftermath, if he loses. This is as long as he's actually done enough previously to at least put himself in the best possible position to win.

Despite feeling in control, the fighter simultaneously leaves the outcome to the decision of fate, or 'God', as many fighters like to rationalise it as. The state of productive pain that a fighter must have experienced becomes healthy when the mind knows that the fighter has sacrificed for the result he wants.

There are four types of sacrifice that a fighter must experience to achieve this state of fearlessness:

Sacrifice of Time

Mastery of boxing skills takes literally years and years of going to the gym every day, day in and day out. Many fighters, who became world champions, or Hall of Famers, first started fighting at a very young age. Most of them started training before they have even started puberty.

Inevitably, what does this mean? Dedicating your whole life to boxing means you will miss out on opportunities to have pleasurable experiences elsewhere. This may be with friends, with family and even just personal activities which you like to do for yourself.

However, by sacrificing time to advance in boxing, you help to provide evidence for your mind so it can justify why the fear of losing is unnecessary. As a potentially great boxer, you need to dedicate thousands of hours to your craft before you will attain the status of a master.

On a smaller level, you need to commit to giving many hours in the boxing gym up until fight night, so that your mind can produce further incentive to look out for the factors which will help you to think positively. The more time spent in the gym and less time spent away from unproductive activities, the better state your mind will be in.

Physical Sacrifice

A fighter's body is broken down, and repeatedly rebuilt, as he pushes his physical limits each time he trains. Obviously, the more you train hard, the better shape you will be in, making it less likely that you will suffer from fatigue inside the ring. So naturally, it makes sense that fighters dedicate most of their time to focusing on pushing their bodies to the limit.

However, physical pain is healthy for not just the regrowth of muscles, but also the regrowth of the mind's confidence. If a fighter does not train significantly hard, he will always be conscious of the fact in the back of his mind that he could have done more. This will create the impression in his mind that there is a larger possibility for defeat.

Consequently, it becomes easier for him to manifest the defeat as we've discussed earlier. This explains why a fighter needs to experience sufficient amounts of physical pain. For as long as the fighter does not push himself past the limit of injuries (which will actually reverse the intended result and cause him to be cautious), then experiencing the post-workout pains in the muscles will instil a fighter with confidence, as he thinks about his own dedication to his training regime.

Sacrifice of Good Emotions

On the pursuit of greatness, many bumps in the road will be encountered. As previously stated before, resilience and the ability to adapt is necessary. This is because you are guaranteed to run into negative situations and challenging scenarios. You will be put into difficult periods of adversity, and you will suffer from frustrating setbacks.

All of these occurrences will arouse negative emotions in you, such as discouragement, doubts, and worries. All of these feelings will be unpleasant to you, adding to the 'costs' of trying to find success in the sport of boxing. However, the more you can come through the bouts of negative emotions after the challenging situation has passed, the more mental evidence you will have that you have sacrificed and invested into the possibility of victory.

An extreme example of this is when Cus D'Amato died, and Mike Tyson continued his career with no rest period. Mike used his feelings of grief to propel him into an emotional state of pride and honour. He vowed even more intensely that he had to complete the mission of winning the championship belt. He would go on to win the heavyweight championship at the young age of 20 years old, a record that stands to this day.

Surrender to the Entitlement of Success

Committing to sacrificing is impossible before a fighter has made the decision in his mind that he definitively believes that boxing is his purpose before anything else. Too many fighters are conflicted, in terms of their clarity of about what they want out of life. You must sacrifice yourself to the huge responsibility of believing that you must act like a champion at all times.

Of course, acting and thinking like a champion means to invest as much as you can into your training and progress. As an ambitious fighter, you need to first believe in your potential to succeed, if you want to achieve your desires and dreams. If you don't, then you will not feel that there is a need to commit to it with conviction. And it is impossible to achieve anything without conviction. Surrendering to the idea of success is a sacrifice.

Once that executive mental decision has been made in your mind, the next step for you is to absolutely pursue this dream with tunnel vision and focus. Once you are subject to that great responsibility, you will find that it weighs heavy on your shoulders. This is because with great responsibility, comes the potential for great guilt when you do not act like the champion you've decided that you are. Your life will be consumed by the task of becoming successful.

For example, if you decide that you have the quality to become a champion, each time you do not act like a champion, you will feel guilty about that decision. Surrendering to the entitlement of success is a huge responsibility. But if you act as a champion for the majority of the time, then prior to a match you will feel more confident about your chances of winning.

Anxious Anticipations of the Athlete

D'Amato on his methods of mentally preparing amateurs leading up to the fight:

"I tell them the first time they're going to fight, the night before they probably won't sleep.

I can't offer them any consolation other than the fact that **the other guy went through the same thing**."

"And when they get down to the fight and enter the dressing-room, especially if they're in an amateur fight, the room is full of possible opponents, because they don't know who they're going to fight.

And **everybody looks calm, confident** and smiling and all the **new boy is aware of is that terrible thump in his chest**, and he's intimidated by their attitude and their confidence."

"What he doesn't realize is that they look at him and they see the same thing in him as he sees in them, because by an exercise of discipline he also puts on a superficial appearance of confidence."

"We go on now into the ring. Half the time they're walking when they go down to the ring as though they're going to the gallows.

So when they climb those stairs, I never call a fighter yellow. Knowing what he goes through, the very act of climbing into that ring stamps him a person of courage and discipline."

"So now they get into the ring. The **other guy probably looks bigger, and stronger and better conditioned** and real muscular and when he starts to loosen up he looks more experienced.

This is the **novice fighter's mind and imagination exaggerating everything**, which is what the mind does."

"**Nothing is ever as bad as the imagination makes it, not even death.**

A person **doesn't realize what's making him nervous unless he understands why he's getting scared**, which is the natural, normal thing. When he understands it he accepts it as such.

Then it doesn't become as intimidating, which is the reason why I take the boy step by step until actually the bell rings to fight."

"I take them that way so that hopefully by the time they get to fight **they've experienced these different feelings** which are often intimidating by themselves.

[They can say] 'Cus said it was going to be like this,' so that they don't feel they are inferior **or less prepared than their opponent**."

"Now, when they go in and face the opponent and the bell rings, for the first time they're facing reality, and suddenly a **relative calmness** comes over them.

Relative. They're still scared but it isn't that terrible intimidating unknown thing"

"But the moment the blows start to be thrown, the effort to throw punches has begun**, he gets calm**, because now this is something he's been prepared to cope with."

"However, I should add that at **no time does fear disappear. It's just as bad in the hundredth fight as it was in the first**, except by the time he reaches a hundred fights or long before that he's **developed enough discipline where he can learn to live with it**, which is the objective, to learn to live with it."

"A man who's thinking or **worried about getting hit is not gonna have a good sense** of anticipation. He will in fact get hit."

"And most importantly, when you get hit you [can] get excited. When you get hit, your head comes up with your hands, when you get hit, that's when you gotta be calmest! "

Philosophy

A Calm Mind Is Logical

With the obvious realisation that stepping into the ring potentially could lead to a loss or a health risk, it is natural for a fighter to feel a lot of anxiety before the match starts. On the day of the fight, your levels of anxiety will be at an all-time high, compared to the rest of the training camp. This is because the daunting reality of the fight is now upon you, and you are anxious to perform and secure the victory.

A large part of why you may feel anxious on the day of the fight is because as you are waiting for match time to start, you have a very small degree of control over the situation at that point. All the training and physical preparation has been done and there is no longer any progress that could be made that would make a large difference.

At this point, you will wander to yourself, whether you have done enough, and other insecurities may come out. As these insecurities come to the forefront, the way you view the world becomes irrational. And as Cus said, this explains why you may look at other fighters around you as being more capable or physically intimidating than you.

However, if a boxer starts fighting with that same frame of mind, it will be extremely difficult for him to relax and fight up to all of his potential. Cus understood that it was essential for a fighter to find ways to deal with the chaotic nature of the mind before a fight.

When faced with stressful situations, it is highly likely that you start to lose your ability to think logically. As Cus believed, a fighter who cannot think in a calm manner inside the ring will increase his chances of being hit by his opponent. In many ways, the mind is justified in its dramatic perception of the risks we may encounter inside the boxing ring. However, thinking in this way will prevent you from being able to fight in a relaxed state.

The reason why being relaxed is important is because it is likely that you will perform better. Your punches will come effortless, and you will make intelligent decisions without mentally tiring yourself. This can only happen if there is less inner friction and tension in your brain to deal with. When there is less tension in the mind, the lack of stress allows your brain to work with more creativity and more flow. This is often what the world of sports and athletics refer to as being in the zone.

The zone is a mental state where performance levels are higher, yet with less energy and effort expended. The most destructive performances of a fighter, where he lands 'at will' and seems to avoid being hit easily, will usually come from a result of that fighter being in 'the zone'.

Before we can manipulate and manage the mind, to even have a chance of being in the zone, we must first understand the mechanics of the mind. As with fear, pre-fight anxiety is a normal trait which every single boxer in the history of the sport has 'suffered' from. The aim for you is not to learn how to try and remove this suffering. Rather, you simply want to accept these feelings and allow them to pass so that there is no tension.

Anxiety often comes from anticipation of an unpredictable threat which we have little control over. We are unsure of what is going to happen, yet we feel as if we cannot do much to change the situation. This is why sacrifice is particularly important, as we discussed in the chapter of fear.

If a fighter feels extremely prepared for the fight, he can use rationale to calm his nerves, knowing that he has left little to chance, and exercised some control to a degree. However, despite this, the mind can still be irrational when you are anxious before a fight.

In this state of irrationality, the fighter's mind has a negative perception of the world around him. He will exaggerate the level to which he perceives the threats around him, as we discussed in the previous chapter. Like many things in life, the wait for something can be unbearable for many, more so than the actual activity itself. Therefore, a fighter needs to develop the ability to help him deal better with the long wait before the fight. Otherwise, he may get into the ring and fail to perform to the best of his abilities.

What can a fighter do to control his mental reactions to anticipation?

Expectancy

Anxiety has a lot to do with the fact that you are uncertain of what is going to happen next. The mind is always fearful of terrain that is unpredictable, which is why Cus stressed the importance of explaining exactly what the fighter will experience in the ring before he steps in. The more they felt they knew what was going to happen next, the more reason they had to feel comfortable about the setting that they were in.

Experience becomes a major key for a fighter as he grows accustomed to the 'routine' of preparing for a fight. The process becomes familiar to you as you gain more experience. This allows you to have the chance to learn how to be in control of your anxieties.

More importantly, a fighter learns that the experience of fighting isn't as bad as he previously perceived it to be. For you to heighten your level of expectancy before one of your own fights, **visualisation** is a powerful mental tool that you can use to make the mind feel familiar with the process. Frequently visualising every aspect of what is to come, from weeks before the bout won't totally eliminate the anxiety. But it will help to add some comfort when the time comes. A fighter should visualise absolutely as many details as he possibly can.

Visualise the walk to the ring, what you will be feeling as you get your hand wrapped, how you will pace along the ring's perimeter as the introductions are underway, and how you will look into your opponent's eyes as the instructions are given. You can also visualise what will happen when the fighting actually starts. Imagine how you will throw your jab magnificently, and how you will defend yourself from your opponent with coolness and calmness. There is never too much that a fighter can positively visualise.

Presence

Unpredictability can be a major cause of anxiety when waiting. But the more conscious a fighter can be to what is presently happening in that exact moment, the more it can actually heighten the senses. The uncertainty of what is going to happen next can actually be more of a reason for you to not focus on what will happen later. Rather, you can be motivated to focus on what is happening *right now* to prevent anything bad happening later.

Logically, even if you do imagine what could happen next, you can't actually definitively say for sure that you know it will happen. Therefore, stressing over it is actually of no use. Focusing all of your sensual awareness on the present moment encourages you to make judgements only on what is currently happening, rather than what could happen. This approach can eliminate anxieties, as you stop worrying about the future, which you have no control over.

Cus believed that once the punches were starting to be thrown in a fight, this could often lead to an increase in your abilities. That is because you are forced to focus on what is happening *now*, right that second. Senses such as sight, feeling and even the sense of hearing can be extremely significant for a fighter as he fights.

When a fighter is experiencing the world through his body/senses, he is no longer excessively connecting with his mind. This is important in eliminating anxieties because worries and doubts start solely from the mind. If a fighter partially disconnects from his mind, then the fighter is also partially disconnected to the negative thoughts that exist in the mind.

To limit your anxieties before a fight, what are some methods a fighter could do to be 'present to the moment'?

Focused breathing or other focused activities will regularly help a fighter to subconsciously live in his senses more easily prior to the fight. Meditative activities refer to when a person focuses all his attention on a particular sense, and experiences his environment through that particular sense.

For example, if a fighter is in the dressing room and he listens to music, he is focusing his attention on the sense of hearing. This takes him out of the place in his mind where doubts may exist. Focused breathing and other 'focused' activities also help the fighter to simply relax.

Focused breathing itself means to calmly breathe in and out, while also focusing your sensual attention to the actual sensation of breathing (the air going in and out, or the movement of his chest etc.). A fighter should regularly practice putting himself in quietly relaxed states. This can be done sitting or lying down. The more you do it, the more it will be easier to get into the relaxed state.

It is widely stated that after eight weeks of focused breathing for 5+ minutes, a person starts to see the mental benefits that come from this practice. While doing so, you should attempt to prevent yourself from focusing on the thoughts that come into your mind. You should let them pass through and stay 'focused' on the breathing.

Other meditative activities that encourage you to live through your senses include listening to music, shadowboxing, body stretching, socialising with peers, or reading. The activities which turn out to have the best effect on a fighter will depend on his temperament and personality. So test out different meditative activities to find out which works best for you.

One of the best ways to enter the zone and eliminate anxiety in the present moment is to simply **make the decision to 'go for it'**, choosing to go even deeper into the present action, regardless of any worries in your mind. This forces you out of your anxious mind and into your body in such a way that you are forced to ignore any unnecessary worries.

You can do this by physically exaggerating whatever it is you're doing, which forces you into the state where you are forced to shed any worries about the outcome. You commit entirely to what you are doing, staying engaged with the process.

For example, if you are warming up in the ring but you take up little space while doing so, you may stay in an anxious state. The solution would then be to raise the stakes, by warming up more intensely, not being afraid to take up massive amounts of space. This could simply mean to walk around the perimeter of the ring. The reasoning for this is because you cannot think or even feel yourself into 'feeling'.

You can only act yourself into feeling. If you physically act as the champion, doing as the elite champion would, you will be more likely to perform as one. Do such actions over time, and you will automatically start thinking like a champion.

Positive Perception

There are two mental zones which a fighter can think from: either **a positive mental zone or a negative mental zone**. The way a fighter thinks, feels, and perceives the world will be strongly affected by which zone he operates from.

It is common knowledge but uncommonly practised, that what you think is what you are. A fighter is the sum of his thoughts that occupy his mind on a daily basis. If a fighter decides to actively allow negative thoughts to run rampant in his mind, he will be operating from a negative mental zone.

In a negative state, it is easier to interpret everything that happens to you as bad, with everything working against you. However, if you are thinking from a positive mental zone, you will interpret the exact same things as being in your favour. This makes it easier to look out for opportunities in training and openings in a fight.

In order to think from a positive mental zone, a fighter should have an endless stream of positive self-affirmations running through his mind at every hour of the day. You should talk up your own potential, complimenting yourself and recognising the beauty of your own qualities. Make efforts to always talk positively with confidence no matter what situation you find yourself in.

You need to be watchful of the words you use to describe your feelings and thoughts. For example, instead of using words like you 'hope' to be a champion, or 'might' be, say you 'know' you will be. Instead of saying a sparring session didn't go well, talk about what did go well and what you learnt, being conscious of the selection of words you use.

In every situation, you should be able to define the positives of any situation. Use words that empower and motivate you, always reminding yourself of your championship potential. In this way, you abide by Cus' philosophy that a fighter should be aware of his qualities. Otherwise, they will count for nothing.

You need to start recognising your own value and worth. You will develop a natural and automatic response to various situations, being able to interpret them as positive, rather than automatically looking for the negative features of a situation. Thinking from this positive mental zone won't just help to relieve you of unnecessary nerves leading up to bouts.

It will also increase your mental stamina as the match goes by and your physical endurance starts to run low. This is because you will have a deep belief in yourself that you are the type of person who is attracted to the certainty of winning.

A positive mental state makes it easier to persevere because you believe you will get a positive result. When you are faced with situations that other fighters would interpret as impossible to come back from, you, on the other hand, will reject the notion of losing. This will come from your ability to believe in your ability to find a way to win, even if that seems to be out of reach to others.

Remarkables Rise to Resistance

Cus on not succumbing to the harsh demands of a grand task:

"Losers are winners who quit, even if you lose, **you still win if you don't quit**"

"When two men are fighting, what you're watching is more a **contest of wills** than of skills, with **the stronger will usually overcoming skill**. The skill will prevail only when it is so superior to the other man's skill that the will is not tested"

"It is the mark of a **great fighter when he has character plus skill.**"

"A fighter with character and skill **will often rise and beat a better fighter** because of this.

"Character is that quality upon which you can depend under pressure and other conditions.

Character makes the fighter predictable. **Character helps him win.**"

"As many times as you see a fellow get tired in the course of a fight, note that **he gets tired when pressure builds** up, after he gets hurt or he's been in some kind of doubtful situation, not being able to control the situation. That's when he starts getting tired."

"That's why when two good fighters get to fight, they're head to head, so to speak, they won't give an inch and they're using all their skills and ability, until maybe about the seventh or eighth or ninth round, **one fighter start to visibly weaken."**

"It [his tiredness] only means he's reached **a point where he no longer can stand the pressure.**

He's now become dominated, because when two people fight it's very much like two armies. **They seek to impose their will** on one another."

"**Break your opponent's will.** Constant attack, no let up. **Destroy his spirit.**"

On the importance of a fighter rising to the challenge without being hindered by his emotions:

"I believe a man is **a professional** when he can **do what needs to be done no matter how he feels within.**"

"An amateur is **an amateur in his attitude emotionally.**

A professional is a professional in the **way he thinks and feels and in his ability** to execute under **the most trying conditions.**"

"The ability to **do what needs to be done regardless of the pressure** and do it with poise, with no reflection of his inner feeling or conflict if it exists, is what makes a professional.

It **has nothing to do with their knowledge.** I'll show you many amateurs with far superior knowledge and ability than top professionals."

On what it takes to be able to rise to the occasion inside the ring:

"**When you get hit that's when you've got to be calm**. A professional fighter has to learn how to hit and not get hit, and at the same time be exciting.

That's what professional boxing is about. You've got to be clever, you've got to be smart, and not get hit, and when you're able to do this, you're a fighter."

Perhaps Cus' most famous quote was his reference to the feelings of the hero and the coward:

"I tell my kids, what is the **difference between a hero and a coward**?

It's only **what you do** which makes the difference. They **both feel the same**. They both fear dying and getting hurt."

"The **hero is more disciplined** and he fights those feelings off and he does what he has to do. **But they both feel the same, the hero and the coward**.

"What is the difference between **being yellow and being brave**? **No difference**."

"The man who is yellow refuses to face up to what he's got to face."

"People who watch you **judge you on what you do, not how you feel**."

Philosophy

Resistance Measures Your Greatness

Cus believed that one of the best predictors of whether a fighter will be a future elite was if he had the ability to 'rise to the occasion', as he put it. This was one of the features which he could assess when he first watched a fighter sparring. Even if the fighter was being outclassed, mainly due to an obvious lack of experience and skill, Cus was able to read that fighter's willingness to try and overcome the punches he was taking.

This was most likely one of the biggest factors that encouraged Cus D'Amato to say 'he will be the next great heavyweight champion', after watching the young Mike Tyson spar for literally just 3 rounds in the early 80's.

Cus believed that a fighter's capability and willingness to resist the prospect of being defeated was the hallmark of every great fighter. Every fighter who believes that he wants to be great should know this: the level of success you are able to attain, is directly proportionate to the problems you are willing to face and overcome inside the ring. There is no alternative. But it is also important to acknowledge that this is the case outside of the ring too. Fighters are often made to make tough decisions in life as well.

Challenges Are Opportunities

When you look at the careers of great fighters, the most memorable moments of a champion's career is the moments when he came up against a challenge. As an ambitious champion, you should switch your perspective from viewing challenges as a problem to viewing challenges as a golden opportunity.

Challenges give the fighter an opportunity to show championship qualities such as resilience, persistence and determination. The spectators of the sport are able to learn who you are and how far you are willing to go by watching how you interact with challenges. A challenge forces a fighter to increase the level of his skill, bringing the best out of them. In these scenarios, your best is required, and without them, the audience would never actually see the true you.

When a fighter upgrades his level of competition and fights the opponents who are of elite calibre, this tends to be the period when he starts to look less spectacular than before. This is because he is now fighting boxers who are just as talented and skilled as he is.

In order to defeat men of greater calibre, he often needs to search inside for something deeper than what he has initially shown, in both his character and skill set. Therefore, a fighter must become familiar with the act of pushing and persisting through testing trials. This trait is *needed* at the top level when the disparities in class are not so wide. Fortunately for you, this is a quality that can be developed and grown.

Developing the Ability to Rise to Resistance:

Inside The Ring

The gym is the place in which great fighters are made. No one is born great. Some fighters are indeed born (and raised) with greater potential to be great, which is certainly true. This only means that certain fighters have either the natural strengths (which *leads* them to be confident early on in their careers) or the personality type (where they are *already* confident about their ability to attract victories).

However, the ultimate deciding factor which will determine your ability to overcome future challenges is the quality time you spend in the gym. There, you have the chance to harness your skills, but also grow your character to be resilient.

The boxing gym is the only place where you are able to replicate the challenges that you will face inside the boxing ring and improve on how you respond to these challenges. Training itself is the sole act of overcoming a physical challenge over and over again. There are two purposes of repeating a physical task inside the boxing gym.

The first is so that the body is forced to adapt to the task, which is done through activities like working the heavy bag or doing press ups etc. Once you become used to a certain level of exercise, the workout no longer tests your limits. Inevitably, to progress in training, you will increase your reps, sets and numbers of exercises which will then make the workout challenging again. Doing so itself is more than just strengthening your body, it also strengthens your mind because you constantly need to persist through challenges.

You consider quitting and giving up prematurely, but in the end, to get better, you fight through the pain to complete the session with satisfaction. When working out, set the amount of rounds or reps you do. But when it starts to become less challenging, increase the number that you do.

For example, if in a circuit the number of press ups you do is 10, then the next day (or week) it may be 12. Then push again once you become used to it and do 14 the next time. Or if 14 feels like too much, do 13. Small progress is better than no progress. And many times, small progress is better than big progress too because you keep yourself from overtraining.

If you wish to develop the trait of being able to fight through challenges, it must be done with a calm head. The **poker face** is a great method which will help you to practice how to remain cool under pressure. Having a 'poker face' means you need to prevent yourself from showing too much emotion with your facial expressions when you train.

Specifically, you should try to limit how much pain you show you are in while trying to get through the workout. For example, if you are skipping with the rope, you shouldn't show the struggle on your face at the first point that you start to feel pain. It is only when the pain starts to become great that you can use the expression of pain to push you over the edge. But before that point, any excessive expressions of fatigue will start to become a habit. And then you will automatically see the exercise as tougher than it actually is.

The second function of repetitive training is for your mind to have the opportunity to learn how you should respond to physical challenges so that you can hit and not get hit. This is done through activities like sparring or working on the pad mitts with your coach. If one choice does not work, then you can try another way. And you keep trying the different options available to you until you get it right.

For example, imagine that you get in the ring to spar with someone is a great defender of right hands. This is a problem which you will need to decode if you wish to get the better of him. Firstly, you must be aware of the fact that it is actually an *opportunity* to practice. You may try to throw your right hand in certain ways. Perhaps you throw it after the jab, or maybe you try to arch it around the side, amongst other options.

If your opponent still manages to defend your punches, then you can keep trying new ways to land it. Eventually, perhaps you throw it as a lead, without the jab, finding that the lessening of telegraphic cues allows you to land the punch before your opponent can adjust to it. You would then mentally log this success.

A smart fighter would think about why it was a success, which would allow him to replicate the success in the future if faced with a similar opponent/problem. Even in the cases where you cannot intelligently come up with solutions, the very act of displaying the courage to even try and impose your will can result in a turn of events.

Boxing is a skill, so primarily you should try and be intelligent. But if intelligence is not enough, then you should still fiercely defy the prospect of failure by increasing your energy levels. This is what Cus referred to as 'will overcoming skill'. By increasing the pressure you place on your opponent, you can tire him out mentally if he isn't willing to rise to the challenge himself.

The best place to practise being able to 'impose your will' is in sparring. Cus D'Amato believed in getting the best possible sparring partners for his fighters, rather than sparring partners that his fighters knew they could easily handle. In fact, the Cus D'Amato camp didn't even use the word 'sparring partner'. Instead, they used the word 'fighting partner'.

This further induced the reality of the situation. His fighters were ordered to take sparring as serious as they would in a fight, even if they were focusing on the technical aspects of what they were doing in the ring. Doing this helped his fighters to develop the assurance they needed when they actually got in the ring.

They were well aware of the fact that they had already experienced the pressure of having to rise to the challenge. If you wish to get the same results, then you must have the same perspective. Never approach sparring lightly, even when you are not physically at full intensity.

If your sparring partner, or 'fighting partner', is less skilled than you and you do not want to hurt them, it is still necessary to retain the exact same high levels of concentration. That way, when you are in the ring, operating in this way is natural and automatic.

Outside of The Ring

The ring is a place where your ambitious character is projected. The ring is simply the stage, being the perfect platform to showcase your ambitious personality. Therefore, the trait of adapting should be developed outside of the ring also. This will grow the belief in yourself that you are the type of person who can remain confident in the face of great challenges. This way, you can truly be relaxed and avoid overreacting with panic.

The most relevant example of this is the adversities that Mike Tyson faced outside of the ring after he won the championship and Cus D'Amato had passed away. After facing numerous personal problems, Tyson's career started to spiral downwards, and his performances became less effective after the years of torment took its toll.

However, had he been able to overcome those adversities successfully, then it's likely that it would have made him an even better fighter because of it. There are many tough decisions and harsh situations which a fighter could be placed in, which could be considered as adversities. For example, this may include when you are injured, and you are trying to map out a return.

It could be any financial issues, as you negotiate with promoters and deal with contracts. You may need to really assess if becoming successful in the sport is a real possibility for you. Or maybe you need to shuffle your team or eliminate certain people from your life.

The adversity will depend on you. But what is fixed, is the fact that you will be faced with these problems and you must learn to deal with them. The ability to problem-solve and adapt to tough new situations is like a muscle which needs to be trained in the gym. It must constantly be grown and worked on for it to become stronger. This type of 'working out' of the mind is done by remaining calm in the face of threats.

The next time that you are challenged in life, make an effort to prevent it from making a difference to your emotional state. Initially, and depending on the size of the adversity, it will seem incredibly difficult and maybe even impossible. But it is certainly possible. Over time, you will become more accustomed to dealing with problems.

You will also become much better at rationalising to yourself, why the problem doesn't have to define you. When you feel the inner anxiety coming up as you contemplate the problem, take long deep breaths. And affirm to yourself that the problem will pass. Rationalise to yourself that the calmer you are about the situation, the better chances you have of dealing with it. Reframe any problem you are faced with as something that will make you stronger if you are able to prove that you are bigger than the problem itself. It can be overcome.

If you want the capabilities of being able to rise to the adversities you are facing on a consistent basis, then you will need to do intelligently.

Working 'hard' is not always the solution, because many problems in life require smart finesse, as opposed to brute force.

What does it mean to intelligently fix your problems? A champion needs to be able to creatively come up with solutions from a place of cool logic. Make a list of options, with some that seem obvious and others which seem a long shot.

Weigh up the best options by considering the benefits of each option that you have come up with, with the costs and risks that you may endure as a result of each option. This is a much better method for facing your problems, than being overly emotional or automatically rushing to the first option that comes to mind. Consistently done, this will internalise a confidence in your ability to get over the challenges you face outside of the ring.

Leadership

"To see a man **beaten** not by a better opponent but **by himself** is a tragedy."

"You can teach better by **setting examples**, than we do by explaining and talking about them."

"Greatness is not a measure of how great you are but **how great others came to be because of you**."

"I **don't allow** people to intimidate me, for no other reason than **to set an example** for my boxers."

"If you can hit your opponent with two punches, you don't hit him with one. Get off with some bad intentions in there.

Believe in yourself. A guy can feel it if you don't believe in yourself. **Set your mind to make yourself** do it."

Philosophy

Boxing Mastery Is About Doing, Not Just Wanting

When the fighter decides he has the potential to be a great champion, he must understand that this alone isn't actually enough for him to realise great success. The most important factor that will command results is action, not desire or belief alone. Being a champion means to be a leader and actively take control of your life.

A champion isn't someone who wants and wishes. The wants and wishes are simply the engines, which fuels the mileage of action for years until you get to the destination that was initially so far away. The problem for many fighters who do not realise their potential is that they lack this knowledge that there is a process to becoming a champion, and this process requires great enormous amounts of action.

As Cus D'Amato said, the best method of learning was by gaining experience, actually physically doing whatever it is that you want to do. We learn best by watching and then physically practising the act which we wish to learn.

A leader is a master of his fate. So you must steer yourself to success with the knowledge you have learnt from your own experiences. But it is through action that you move towards your goal. And after achieving success yourself, having learnt the process it takes to be successful, you then become an inspiration to others. You are now a clear example to others that share your same desires for life.

But to build yourself into a leader, there are certain traits you must develop so that you can proactively dictate your life:

The Traits of a Leader

Decision-making & conviction

A leader is a person who has a clear understanding of who he is, and he has clarity of intent regarding what he wants out of a situation, or in life. As a champion, you must learn and clearly define what you stand for as a person.

What do you like? What do you dislike? What behaviours will you not tolerate in your life? What morals do you wish to promote? More relevant to boxing, you must learn explicitly what it is that you want out of your career.

Make a plan which specifically outlines how you think these goals will be achieved. And you must think about why you even want to achieve those goals. While identifying and discovering your inner reality, you must actively decide that you accept these qualities about yourself, knowing this is good enough.

You do not have to live up to anyone else's standard of what is good enough. This means to unapologetically stick with what you believe, what you feel, and what you desire, even if it is in conflict with the values of other people. A leader believes in what *he* believes. This mental shift will result in you developing the trait of having conviction in all of your actions. You know who you are and what your goals are.

You will also have an understanding of why these are your goals, which pushes you to dive into action with conviction and commitment. Without commitment and belief in your actions, you will fail to translate your inner reality of desires onto the external world.

Committing to an action will result in revolutionary changes in the environment. No change or influence in the outer world will take place without that stalwart conviction. But once you gain it, the world will seem to be a canvas, which you can paint your own personal art on.

Conviction is especially important in your punches and in all of your technical moves inside the ring. If you half-heartedly throw a punch or hesitate before making a step, you will allow your opponent the chance to take advantage. It is impossible to impose your will on an opponent if you are uncertain or in two minds. Your opponent will fill the gap with his own will.

Train so that you develop conviction in all techniques that you use and have no doubts. This is the reason for constant repetition of the same techniques over and over again. It is so that you develop the assurance that when you do it in a match, you know that it will lead to a positive result, rather than a risk. Work towards developing this trait with your character too. When you speak and state a certain belief, do it with conviction and belief, rather than thinking about whether it is acceptable for others.

When you walk to the ring from the dressing room in front of a crowd of many watching eyes, you can do with conviction and belief. Because you've practised how to shed your mind of allowing the opinions of others to affect you. When you decide to throw a punch at an opponent, you step in with conviction which your opponent starts to feel as the match progresses.

You dominate the direction of the fight at your own will and make 'all his causes a lie'. This is all impossible without a certain level of belief and conviction. From one perspective, acting with conviction is the act of making a decision, and then simply sticking to it. Even in little everyday decisions, you need to be clear in your intent and speak with a tone that reflects confidence.

You need to believe in your actions so much to the extent that you are willing to stand alone in your actions if need be, even in the face of harsh criticism. But facing criticism doesn't mean that you even feel the need to justify your decisions. In fact, you speak less and are more to the point, with a vibe that reflects your inner conviction.

People will start to simply subconsciously feel your confidence. Once you can do this, you are performing as a leader. A leader doesn't feel the need to explain when it's not necessary or backtrack in his beliefs if it isn't liked or approved of. Once outsiders see your own belief in your own world, this will attract followers who become excited by the prospect of also joining your world.

Persistence & Consistency

The road to glory and mastery is a long one. It is a path that weeds out those who are not truly serious about their ambitions. In order to achieve ring success, you will need to be extremely persistent in your training and consistent in match performances.

Persistence in Training

As the young Mike Tyson said, fighting 'is the easy part about fighting because the training is the hard part'. The truth is that training is monotonous and boring naturally. You repeat the same technique and the same workouts literally thousands of times. But it is important to accept that this is the reality of boxing. Boxing mastery requires consistency.

It is important that you are persistent even if you are facing personal problems in your life. Many roadblocks will threaten to derail you from your focus in training. But you need to continue to spend time in the boxing gym. These obstacles can come in the form of distractions, injuries, personal tragedies, financial struggles, rejections, and any other setbacks that slow your progress towards your training targets.

Distractions are the perfect opportunity to test how far you are willing to go for boxing greatness. But what separates the good fighters and the great fighters, is the consistency of discipline throughout these situations. Many fighters fall short of success because they allow their levels of discipline to drop during the darker periods of life. Consequently, they do not gain any momentum to push themselves out of it.

However, a potentially great fighter will remain disciplined by making sure that he still invests hours into training to maintain his progress. If a fighter is injured, does he still progress in his boxing in another way?

I.e. studying fight films, exercising other parts of the body, working on light intensity skill drills etc. If a fighter suffers a bad break up (in a relationship or in another manner), does he allow his depression to keep him out of the gym? Once a fighter starts to make money and gain enormous amounts of attention, is he able to stay level-headed and consistent in the gym? A great champion will use his desire to remain persistent throughout these trials and tribulations.

Obstacles are not just prevalent when it comes to training, but it is also the case when it comes to matches. A fighter should remain consistent with his level of performances at all times, regardless of what is happening outside of the ring, and the issues he may have prior to going in the ring.

Being clear in your purpose helps a fighter to do this, as it forces him to set a standard that he has to live up to. Otherwise, he will fail to strive in accordance with his purpose. You must know what it is you want and why.

Lastly, being consistent in matches refers to the moments when you've been hit and hurt, and have to manage the situation afterwards. As an elite fighter, 'when you get hit, that's when you gotta be calm, remaining 'clever, [and] smart'. Again, you can only select the most logical options to help you come back when you're calm. No matter what happens in the ring, a fighter should stick to his standard emotional bassline. Otherwise, he will be at risk of potentially losing control of his actions and thoughts.

Authenticity & Charisma

Champions are leaders. A leader is a person who has enough belief in himself, and enough inner security in who is as a person and fighter, to live without feeling the need to hide or lie about the traits and qualities that make him the person he is.

Being authentic means to allow your unique traits to be left on display, with no stress put on whether it fits in with what other people perceive as 'normal'. This includes being candid about your flaws and insecurities, as well as your strengths.

Do not focus on trying to project 'perfection', as it does not exist. Cus believed that perfection should only be viewed as a target. We can try to attain it, as this will push us further, giving us the sight of a bigger goal we may want. However, deep down you must keep in mind that once you perfect a particular skill, there will be something else to 'perfect'.

Absolute perfection does not exist. Relative perfection is only a means to help you set targets and be motivated to attain them. 'Perfection is a relative point which once a person reaches it, he then is able to see further ahead than he was able to see before that point. And then, if he has the drive, he becomes what he wants to become because now he sees the possibility of doing it'.

This perspective gives you the perfect rele~~ attachments you have to believe that perfection is e~ certainly not a thing which you put any stress on trying attain the myth of perfection will make it difficult to make mistakes, and take risks. These experiences are needed to learn from.

A fighter cannot develop the quality of leadership without being fully honest about who he is, from the good to the bad. This may seem counterintuitive, but shedding your ego will allow you to become a better champion.

Being honest and forgetting the myth of perfection will also give you the desired trait of charisma, inside and outside of the ring. If a champion can be honest about his character and accepts himself for who he is, he will have the confidence to express his true personality. It also allows him to be humble, which makes the champion more relatable to the fans.

The fans will love him even more so than if he was the person trying to be liked by everyone because he represents the values which they also stand for. In turn for the inspiration he provides, they provide unconditional support for their leader and champion.

A champion will be strongly motivated by his followers, as he starts to understand that he is now acting in the service of many people, rather than just himself. This aids him in his cause of motivation and drive.

In order to develop this quality, you must decide and commit to being truly yourself in all areas. Then you must accept yourself for who are, regardless of what opinions may be formed from others. You must allow this strong sense of personalisation and individuality to flow through your boxing, both inside the ring with how you fight, and also outside of the ring.

For example, your training schedules and preferences must be tailored to your personal desires, rather than what is widely accepted as normal. Perhaps running at night will benefit you *personally*, as opposed to the common belief that it is better to run in the morning. It is about knowing what's right for *you*.

Once you practice applying this to all areas of your boxing and life, issues such as stage fright and crumbling under pressure from the crowd will start to gradually evaporate to a point of little significance.

A Greater Purpose

Cus D'Amato himself is a great example of a leader living what he teaches and teaching what he lives. In the 20th century, with racism still common in society to the point where blacks and whites could not even share the same toilet, Cus D'Amato stood up for the black fighters under his wing.

When Cus D'Amato travelled across the country with his black fighters, his fighters were sometimes not allowed in certain hotels and in certain establishments. Cus would sleep outside with his fighters, despite the fact that he himself was allowed to. Other times when Cus would accommodate people of authority with certain racial prejudices, he would let them know with strictness, that they are to 'treat them with the same respect that you would treat Camille and me'.

For some, this may not seem significant. But in a time where the vast majority were living with racist beliefs that were widely accepted, Cus had enough confidence in his own beliefs to go the other way. This type of stalwart stubbornness in your beliefs is exactly what makes you a leader.

A champion and leader is the 'first among many' when he definitively represents an idea, value or certain culture. Without representing a purpose, he is merely a fighter, regardless of his success.

For many champions, they may represent working hard and pulling themselves out of extreme poverty. For others, it may be representing the country and culture they come from. Or for some, it is making enough money to ensure financial security for your family for generations. What purpose do you want to represent?

The common denominator here is that there is a purpose which is bigger than the champion himself. This is what fans and followers can get behind, as they share the exact same desires that the champion represents and fights for. This is important because a purpose that is bigger than you will motivate you on a much higher level than anything personal ever could.

You are no longer performing for you. You are now forced to a higher standard. It also accelerates your own progress, because if you can be the leader behind a purpose, you will be more confident in yourself.

Conclusion – Final Notes

Being a champion is more than just operating with a particular technique that makes the fighter successful. In fact, any technique that abides by the fundamentals of fighting can be made successful, so long as the fighter has a strong mentality.

Cus D'Amato was the first famous promoter of this concept. Who before him had said they don't teach a kid how to fight until they've spoken to him and shown the kid of his own potential greatness? Cus D'Amato was the first of his kind in this respect.

It has been over 30 years since his passing. But the philosophies and teachings which helped to create his champions, Patterson, Torres and Tyson, live on. And they can be internalised by living everyday with these particular philosophies in mind.

In this book we looked at five different areas that a champion should consciously develop within himself. The five areas were:

- The **character** of the fighter
- How to perceive and deal with **fear**
- How to limit **anxieties**
- Rising to the **resistance** of challenges
- Becoming a **leader**.

Cus D'Amato's quotes are great references to look on and draw inspiration and guidance from. He was a man who underwent many challenges and experiences himself. By taking the lessons he learnt without having to spent time going through the same efforts and experiences, we can learn his lessons quickly.

I implore you to make efforts to live by, and test the trueness of Cus' philosophies. You have an advantage over the rest of the boxing world. This advantage is rooted in the fact that the majority of other fighter's will stick to what is normal.

They won't venture out into the unknown, or go through a path that is different to that of the average path. Consequently, they won't grow the quality of being a champion in the heart and mind as quickly as they possibly could. This is where you can stand alone and make the separation.

By practising the art of acting as a champion, you will automatically be doing what many others will not do. Not only will this give you peace of mind, as well as happiness and contentment in who you are, but it will also make you a better fighter. You will be able to dictate the direction of your fights better, as you become confident enough to naturally dictate your environment at will. You'll be in tune with your belief in who you are, and what you want. And this will transcend your entire environment.

Good Luck,

Reemus

Thank You – Leave A Review Please!

Thank you for purchasing this book!

I hope that the mental strategies and theories that we have discussed in this book have been, and will be, helpful to you and your mental progression in the sport of boxing.

For a long time, since before the days of Cus D'Amato, there has been a need for a focus on this aspect of the sport. But since the legendary Cus D'Amato showed us this, there has been little attention given to this area.

This is despite the fact that every successful person in the sport, including boxers and top coaches, acknowledge that boxing is all mental (for the most part). You can go to the gym to progress physically, but there aren't many sources for a potential champion to go to, to learn how he can manage his mental game.

However, I implore you to be conscious of the fact that not only the body needs training. And your body will go much further if you are able to master your mind. I'd advise you to read, watch and surround yourself with all the material that will help you in this regard.

Other materials on Cus D'Amato which may help you:

Undisputed Truth: My Autobiography - by Mike Tyson (Autobiography)

Iron Ambition: Lessons I've Learned from the Man Who Made Me a Champion - by Larry Sloman and Mike Tyson

  To help bring attention to this cause, and to help other fighters with their mental game, it'd be very helpful if you could leave an informative review on Amazon. If you enjoyed the contents of the book and would like to help the brand grow, which will allow us to release more, extensive content, leave a review!

Thank you so much champ, and good luck!

Stay Connected

Join thousands of fighters and fight fans and follow the brand on social media:

Subscribe on YouTube ('Reemus Boxing') – A media channel which includes the popular 'Art of Boxing' series, where Reemus breaks down the technical skills of boxers and boxing matches. Also included is the 'Champion's Mentality' series and the 'Art of the Champion' series where we look at the past and current boxing champions to study the traits that led to their success. Other content also includes news coverage, classic film overviews and other entertaining boxing related videos.

Follow on Instagram ('@ReemusBoxing') – The media channel which focuses on covering the latest news in boxing and entertaining you with updates on what is going on in the current climate.

Listen to the podcast ('ChampSet') – The Champ-Set podcast is specifically for fighters who want to dive deeper into what champions do to get, and sustain, their success. We go into greater detail on motivational topics and mental strategies to help you be a focused fighter that progresses quicker than everyone else. We also talk about trending topics in the boxing world, and we invite other fighters and fight experts. With no doubt, the most informative podcast in the world for fighters.

Subscribe to the blog newsletter (ReemusBoxing.com) – The boxing blog is focused on three categories: gym training, mental training, and history. From articles on how to throw effective combinations and what equipment to buy, to how you can manage your anxiety and what happened when Jack Johnson took on Jim Jeffries, it can be found on the blog. Subscribe to the newsletter to get updates on the brand (promotional discounts, and video alerts).